# How to tell if You're a REAL Race Fan

## A GUIDEBOOK FOR STOCK CAR FANS

*by Jim McCulloch*

*Illustrations by Raid Ahmad*

*How to tell if you're a REAL Race Fan*
*A guidebook for stock car fans*
**by Jim McCulloch**

Published by: StoneBrook Publishing  P.O. Box 30696  Charlotte, NC  28230

1st Printing, 1996

**Publisher's Cataloging in Publication**
*(Prepared by Quality Books Inc.)*

McCulloch, Jim.
     How to tell if you're a REAL race fan : a guidebook for stock
car fans / by Jim McCulloch ; illustrations by Raid Ahmad.
       p. cm.
       LCCN: 96-67530
       ISBN 0-9651107-2-9

     1. Stock car racing--Humor.   I. Ahmad, Raid, ill.   II. Title

GV1029.9.S74M33 1996              796.7'2
                                              QBI96-20205

# **DEDICATION**

*to my favorite people in the whole world*
*- race fans -*
*thanks for the inspiration!*

To order additional copies of this book
*How to tell if you're a REAL Race Fan*, by Jim McCulloch
send $6.95 (plus 3.00 shipping for the first book
and .50 cents for each additional book) to:

**StoneBrook Publishing**
**P.O. Box 30696**
**Charlotte, NC 28230**

credit card orders call toll-free **1-800-205-8254** anytime
fax orders: 1-602-481-9712
e-mail orders: www.bookzone.com
customer service only: 1-704-849-6878

## How to tell if You're a REAL Race Fan

You've spent more time in autograph lines than you did going to high school

• • •

You've fallen off an RV and didn't get hurt

• • •

You can explain how the point system works but you can't get your checkbook to balance

## How to tell if You're a REAL Race Fan

You bought a souvenir just because it was
a "Limited Edition"

• • •

You always forget where you parked your car

• • •

The longest conversation you've had with your
spouse was about Dale, Rusty or Mark

# How to tell if You're a REAL Race Fan

A driver's birthday is circled on your calendar

# How to tell if You're a REAL Race Fan

It was cheaper to have your car towed than
to pay for infield parking

• • •

Two or more of your children are named Dale

• • •

All the State Troopers directing traffic
on race day know you by name

# How to tell if You're a REAL Race Fan

You've been bruised by your own body parts
while cheering

# How to tell if You're a REAL Race Fan

Every piece of clothing you own has a car number on it

## How to tell if You're a REAL Race Fan

You voted fifty times for Bill Elliott
as "Fan's Favorite Driver"

• • •

You've phoned a crew chief to offer suggestions

• • •

After a race you saw a sign saying
**WET PAVEMENT AHEAD** ...so you did

11

# How to tell if You're a REAL Race Fan

You think race traffic is a good place to meet women

# How to tell if You're a REAL Race Fan

Your new racing tattoo actually improved
your appearance

• • •

The smell of burning tires makes you hungry

• • •

You'd like to own a condo at Charlotte just
so you could moon people

13

# How to tell if You're a REAL Race Fan

You've spent ten dollars on one hamburger and a beer

## How to tell if You're a REAL Race Fan

You've listened to the race on a car radio
during a funeral procession

• • •

*"Ricky, Ricky, Ricky - Sterling, Dale, Mark, Mark"*
is how you remember mom's phone number

• • •

You tried to read the wet newspaper you
found in a port-a-potty

## How to tell if You're a REAL Race Fan

You can say "Dick Trickle" outside of a doctor's office without fear of embarrassment

• • •

Your date dented the roof of your car during a race

• • •

You think the *"Fab Four"* were
Bobby, Donnie, Neil and Davey

# How to tell if You're a REAL Race Fan

Your brother's favorite driver always wrecks yours

## How to tell if You're a REAL Race Fan

Track announcer Bill Connell has nearly sent you into cardiac arrest at least twice

• • •

You got married on an "off" weekend

• • •

Despite the deafening roar of forty thundering cars, you still yell at the top of your lungs, "WHERE'D YOU LEARN TO DRIVE, YOU IDIOT?"

# How to tell if You're a REAL Race Fan

Your sofa has more than five decals on it

## How to tell if You're a REAL Race Fan

You cheer while watching tapes of
races you've seen before

• • •

If you've ever said,
"What debris? I don't see no dang debris!"

• • •

You know if *you* were a driver, you'd
win the Championship

# How to tell if You're a REAL Race Fan

If you've forgotten to put sunscreen on your belly

# How to tell if You're a REAL Race Fan

Your riding lawn mower is painted like a race car

## How to tell if You're a REAL Race Fan

After a race you can't identify the goo
between your toes

• • •

Your Christmas card photo is you
in front of a race car

• • •

You eat at a restaurant thirty straight days
hoping to see Jeff and Brooke again

# How to tell if You're a REAL Race Fan

Your mama washed *your* mouth out with soap
after listening to your race scanner

## How to tell if You're a REAL Race Fan

The only time you've been on TV, you pointed to your cap and hollered, "Yeaaaahhhh!"

• • •

You gave front row tickets to your ex-boss for his first race

• • •

The T-shirt you wear to the race is also your pajamas

# How to tell if You're a REAL Race Fan

Airline pilots have demanded lights be put on the racing flagpole in your yard

## How to tell if You're a REAL Race Fan

You've offered to trade your spouse
for a garage pass

• • •

You can name the top ten drivers in a single belch

• • •

The "Daytona or Bust" painted on your car
won't wash off

## How to tell if You're a REAL Race Fan

If you've ever said, "This autograph ain't for me,
it's for my, ... uh, ... nephew."

• • •

You thought *"Days of Thunder"* was realistic

• • •

You've called a TV station to report
seeing Elvis in the infield

# How to tell if You're a REAL Race Fan

You got up early to beat traffic and then
slept through half the race

## How to tell if You're a REAL Race Fan

You've got more than one racing cap in
the rear window of your car

• • •

You wet your pants when you
finally met Bill Elliott

• • •

At home, you listen to the race on your radio headset
during TV commercials

# How to tell if You're a REAL Race Fan

Your best shirt is covered with driver autographs

# How to tell if You're a REAL Race Fan

You draft behind trucks on the Interstate

## How to tell if You're a REAL Race Fan

If you've ever turned to a total stranger and said,
"Now that's what I call a loose rear end!"

• • •

Your garage is full of racing magazines

• • •

You fall asleep thinking about Cindy Crawford
but dream about Benny Parsons

## How to tell if You're a REAL Race Fan

A caution flag waves and you immediately
look for Jimmy Spencer

• • •

Monday you don't really "wake up"
as much as "come to"

• • •

You've sat in a lawn chair yelling,
"I THINK I'M IN LOVE!"

# How to tell if You're a REAL Race Fan

You've worn sunglasses and a cowboy hat trying
to look like the King

# How to tell if You're a REAL Race Fan

It's days after the race and you're *still* finding chicken bones in your hair

# How to tell if You're a REAL Race Fan

You've had your picture taken next to
a cardboard stand-up

## How to tell if You're a REAL Race Fan

You routinely pay more than four times the
normal hotel room rate

. . .

You anonymously sent Kyle a pair of scissors

. . .

You once had "Bubba" paged at the track
just to watch the stands empty

# How to tell if You're a REAL Race Fan

It takes more than three people to lift your cooler

## How to tell if You're a REAL Race Fan

You've used your own underwear and
pretended to be Doyle Ford

• • •

You stay in the same Daytona hotel every year

• • •

You've driven alongside a team's hauler on the
highway just to wave madly

# How to tell if You're a REAL Race Fan

You dress formally to stay home and watch
the New York award banquet on TV

## How to tell if You're a REAL Race Fan

You need a full length mirror to see your
latest driver autograph

• • •

If every caution flag means a game of horseshoes

• • •

The most romantic night of your life was spent in a
rental car parked next to the Daytona infield lake

# How to tell if You're a REAL Race Fan

You've shaved a car number into the hair on your back

# How to tell if You're a REAL Race Fan

You gave your wife a die-cast car for an
anniversary gift

## How to tell if You're a REAL Race Fan

You didn't stop that obnoxious fan who thought
your tobacco-juice spit cup was his beer

• • •

You holler at the TV announcers during a race

• • •

You always wear your lucky racing T-shirt
to job interviews

# How to tell if You're a REAL Race Fan

Your most cherished possession is a lug nut that flew into the stands and broke your nose

## How to tell if You're a REAL Race Fan

The lottery numbers you pick are always the top
six finishers in last week's race

• • •

This is the first racing book you've actually read

• • •

You always dress your kids for Halloween
as the Bodine brothers

# How to tell if You're a REAL Race Fan

You think fireworks are required to camp in the infield

## How to tell if You're a REAL Race Fan

You've been thrown off a golf course for
reckless cart driving

• • •

After a race there's enough grit on your face
to clog the sink

• • •

You have the top five scores on the
racing video game at the mall

## How to tell if You're a REAL Race Fan

You'd give a week's pay for a date with one of those Victory Lane babes

• • •

The stains on the jeans you wore to Talladega have sentimental value to you

• • •

You mistakenly went into a gay bar after hearing about a "pole position party"

# How to tell if You're a REAL Race Fan

You can chew and cheer at the same time

51

## How to tell if You're a REAL Race Fan

Pretending to be in victory lane, you once soaked your living room with warm beer

• • •

People on pit road make fun of the way you dress

• • •

You sent a wedding invitation to a driver and were actually disappointed he didn't show

# How to tell if You're a REAL Race Fan

Your dog is named after your favorite driver

# How to tell if You're a REAL Race Fan

You got stuck trying to climb in the driver's
side window of your own car

• • •

You often apologize by saying, "But dear, someday
this will be worth a fortune."

• • •

After you called in sick to work, your boss
saw you at qualifying

# How to tell if You're a REAL Race Fan

You hate foreign-made cars

# How to tell if You're a REAL Race Fan

You call a souvenir company demanding your name be put ON their mailing list

• • •

There's crumpled sheet metal in your bedroom

• • •

You wake up to find your infield campsite surrounded by yellow police tape

# How to tell if You're a REAL Race Fan

You've burned a hole in a U-Haul truck

# How to tell if You're a REAL Race Fan

You've left a family member at home because
there wasn't room for them *and* the beer

## How to tell if You're a REAL Race Fan

If you've worn a cardboard sign that read,
"SHOW ME UR BOOBS"

• • •

Your die-cast car collection is worth more
than your real car

• • •

You recorded a race over the videotape of
your latest wedding

# How to tell if You're a REAL Race Fan

The legs on your coffee table are used race tires

## How to tell if You're a REAL Race Fan

When you tried to drive with one eye closed like
Ernie, you ran over the neighbor's cat

• • •

The first car out of a race is always the one you bet on

• • •

You still haven't washed your hand after shaking
Ned Jarrett's last year in Daytona

61

# How to tell if You're a REAL Race Fan

You got in a fight with your mother-in-law over
which driver is better-looking

## How to tell if You're a REAL Race Fan

The hot new racing collectible is the same idea
you had two years ago

• • •

You've used ear plugs you found on the ground

• • •

You framed a photo of yourself and a driver
who has no idea who you are

# How to tell if You're a REAL Race Fan

You've put your favorite recliner
on top of a van

## How to tell if You're a REAL Race Fan

You've discreetly dropped popcorn down the crack
of a fat guy sitting in front of you

• • •

If you've used a concession stand hose for a shower

• • •

You rush home early to see the TV highlights
of the race you just left

## How to tell if You're a REAL Race Fan

You'll buy anything if there are
collectible driver cards inside

• • •

You've taken a transistor radio to church

• • •

If you've ever paid $20 to park in
somebody's front yard

# How to tell if You're a REAL Race Fan

You got ink all over yourself trying to duplicate
Richard Petty's autograph

## How to tell if You're a REAL Race Fan

The biggest loudmouth at the race always
sits right behind you

• • •

You don't pack underwear for a race weekend

• • •

In your neighborhood, you're known as "the guy
with his transmission stuck in neutral"

You freshen your race day breath by gargling beer

## How to tell if You're a REAL Race Fan

Your idea of "getting away from it all" includes
fifty thousand other people

• • •

You know a shortcut to every track

• • •

Your wife wakes you every morning by screaming,
"TROUBLE IN TURN ONE!"

Without all the bumper stickers your
bumper would fall off

## How to tell if You're a REAL Race Fan

You think the rules *obviously* favor the:
☐ Chevys    ☐ Fords    ☐ Pontiacs

• • •

You belong to at least four Driver Fan Clubs

• • •

On your next honeymoon you *will* make it
to the Dawsonville Pool Room

# How to tell if You're a REAL Race Fan

Your grandmother once beat up a guy for not removing his hat during the National Anthem

## How to tell if You're a REAL Race Fan

You've pretended to be a spotter getting a driver safely through a wreck

• • •

You bring a stopwatch to the track

• • •

You always buy a T-shirt of the race winner to wear over the one you bought last week

# How to tell if You're a REAL Race Fan

If you've left a car idling in race traffic while you ran to pee in the bushes

## How to tell if You're a REAL Race Fan

If you've driven around a neighborhood
looking for "his" house

• • •

You've been knocked senseless by
someone waving a cap

• • •

You like being at the race because
nobody can hear you fart

# How to tell if You're a REAL Race Fan

Jumping up to
see a wreck, you once
accidentally swallowed
an entire corn dog

You make race car sounds in swivel chairs at work

## How to tell if You're a REAL Race Fan

Just for fun you call all the Earnhardts in the
phone book at 2:00 a.m.

• • •

You've lost a bet on a track-drying vehicle

• • •

You can name all your favorite driver's kids,
but not your own

# How to tell if You're a REAL Race Fan

You do all your
Christmas shopping
at souvenir trailers